THE MEDITERRANEAN

Leslie Gardiner

FAMILY LIBRARY
of
WORLD TRAVEL

The Acropolis of Athens: showground of the golden age *previous page.* The temple is the Parthenon, or 'virgin palace'. The rocky plateau where it stands with other marvels of Greece's golden age (450—400 BC) is the Acropolis, the citadel of Athens. The hill on the right is the Lycabettus, strangely unmentioned in classical literature.

Pisa's leaning miracle. Built around 1360 AD, like the adjacent Baptistery, the Romanesque bell-tower of Pisa is falling. Earth movements and its own weight are exaggerating the initial tilt and the top is now 13 feet off-center. The Italian Government offers a rich prize for a solution to the subsidence.

First Published in 1985
for AGT Publishing
by Octopus Books Limited
59 Grosvenor Street
London W1, England

© 1985 Octopus Books Limited

ISBN 0-933521-17-0

Produced by Mandarin Publishers Ltd
22a Westlands Road
Quarry Bay, Hong Kong

Jacket Photography: Zefa Picture Library

CONTENTS

INTRODUCTION

'Mediterranean' means 'middle of the earth', and the ancient civilizations that lived around its shores had no doubt that it was. They regarded the countries on its boundaries (Italy, Greece, Palestine, Egypt, Carthage) as the extent of the civilized world, and believed that beyond them were lands of savage tribes and mythical beasts, unknown and unimportant.

When the cruise ship sails through the Straits of Gibraltar (once the Pillars of Hercules), it enters the classical world. The reality does not disappoint the mental picture most people have of the Mediterranean. There are mild skies, water shading from turquoise to ultramarine according to depth, and white towns on the shore. These regions hold the foundations of our cultural traditions, our laws and political systems and religions – Judaic, Christian or Moslem. This is the stage, with its shifting historical backcloth, on which the dramas of 30 centuries have been played.

A tour of the Mediterranean by boat is quite short. You cannot be out of sight of land for long. In the course of a day you pass from Italy to Greece, while another day and a half takes you to Israel or Egypt. An Italian island is visible from both Tunis and the Italian mainland, and the voyage from Tunis to Morocco takes only two days. By air, all these journeys take minutes rather than hours.

'Prick this earth with a needle and you uncover the bones of heroes' – that was said of Greece, but it applies to most of the lands with which this book deals. The whole area is a dense concentration of strikingly different ancient cultures, brilliant with the highlights of world history. It is amazing that a collection of relatively small countries, gathered within such narrow limits, should have developed in such individualistic ways. Antiquities and the whole cultural heritage of one great ancient civilization – that of the Nile valley in Egypt – are quite different from the antiquities and heritage of Greece. And the 'glory that was Greece' is as different again from the 'grandeur that was Rome'. There were also smaller civilizations which appeared briefly before vanishing mysteriously, such as the Etruscans in Italy, the Minoans of Crete, the Phoenicians of Tunisia, the Nubians and Berbers of the deserts.

If there were no historic ruins, we would still flock to the Mediterranean shores for the scenery. The islands and gulfs of Greece and the lakes and mountains of Italy are the regions to which even the masters of the ancient world retired. In Israel and Egypt fertile vales contrast splendidly with awesome rocky deserts. The evergreen coasts and forested mountain ranges of Morocco and the broad, colored beaches and delicious climate of Tunisia are bringing those two countries rapidly into the forefront of Mediterranean touring programs.

The Riddle of the Sands. Mind-boggling in size and artistry, the Egyptian Sphinx ('strangler') with lion's body and Pharaonic head guards the Nile valley near Cairo. Along with the neighboring Giza pyramids it symbolizes the might and majesty of Nile civilization 5000 years ago. The Sphinx is the focal point of the son et lumière show performed after dark. Seated below the Sphinx, visitors listen to a narrative about Egypt's history, illustrated with powerful colored lights.

The Colosseum: Rome's grandeur in picturesque decay. Built 72–79 AD, the Colosseum held 50,000 spectators on many a Roman holiday. Wild-beast shows and combats between gladiators took place (lions and Christians met elsewhere), and the arena could be flooded for battles with model warships.

ITALY

Rome • Venice • Florence
Milan • Pisa • Genoa
Verona • Pompeii • Sicily

W orld travelers keep a special place in their affections for Italy. This is more than a superb vacationland, it is an affair of the heart. When thinking of Italy, a confusion of images arises. These images may be of Alpine peaks and fast-flowing milky torrents, of shimmering lakes bordered with villas and oleanders, of the misty poplars of the Lombardy plain, or of rose-bricked towers in Tuscany and pantiled cottages which hang precariously from Calabrian cliffs.

Memorable sights include gondolas on Venetian canals, the mosaics of Ravenna and the bullet-domes of Palermo, the striped belfries of Florence and the chalk-white statues and arches of Rome. Those who venture further afield will recall bullock-wagons carrying wine barrels, swaying along under the cypress avenues of Chianti country, and almond trees in blossom among the beehive dwellings of Puglia.

Italy seems to be a land of eternal youth and continual sunshine, so that all these recollections are tinged with a warmth and a softness that is perpetually appealing.

Everyone recognizes the map of Italy by its shape: a long leg under the massive loins of the Alps, terminating in a heel (the department of Puglia) and a sharp toe (Calabria) kicking the tricorne hat of Sicily. To the west, the elongated island of Sardinia has already been kicked halfway to France.

Topographically, such a land cannot fail to be interesting. No place in the peninsula of Italy is more than 50 miles from the sea. On the heights of the Apennines – the chain of granite mountains which runs the length of the peninsula – there are cottages where melting snow from one side of the roofs ends up in the Adriatic Sea and from the other in the Tyrrhenian.

'All roads lead to Rome' is as true today as when the consular roads first radiated from the imperial capital, and the legions marched along them to conquer Europe, North Africa and the Middle East. On all main roads in Italy the distance from Rome is marked every kilometre, as it was then.

'Rome was not built in a day' they say, and this is the magic of the Eternal City: layer upon layer of history has formed it. Rome has something in it to relate to the hopes and interests of all ages, cultures and creeds. It has been the spiritual metropolis of whole nations and

St Peter's Square, Rome: auditorium for the Christian world. Bernini's curving colonnades (1656–67) embrace the thousands who approach St Peter's basilica every day and the half-million who gather on Sundays to receive the papal blessing. There are 284 columns and 88 pillars. A seaman of Bordighera earned his town permanent papal honors for saving the central obelisk from disaster when it was being hoisted in 1586. In the center background is the Tiber, with Ponte Sant' Angelo and the rounded ramparts of Castel Sant' Angelo. In the castle, are museums, armories, a terrace café and the tomb of the Emperor Hadrian who died in 138 AD.

the different stages of its history are still visible – if not on the ground, then in the museum down the street.

Veii, where Etruscan princes lived when Rome was just a ramshackle encampment, now stands within Rome's northern gates. The tomb of Romulus, founder of Rome in 735 BC, is on the Palatine hill and nearby stands the temple where the early Romans stockpiled their weapons. (Ancient writers described how the spears waved and trembled when danger threatened the city.) Remnants of statues and buildings from the time of the Republics and the Emperors are strewn over the Palatine, Capitoline and Celian, three of the seven hills of

St Peter's, Rome: lofty nucleus of the Catholic faith *above*. In 319 AD the Emperor Constantine erected a church over the tomb of the apostle Peter. Twelve hundred years later, Italy's finest artists were employed to transform it into the central basilica of Christendom. The colonnaded approach, Via della Conciliazione, was built by Mussolini to celebrate Rome's peace with the Vatican in the Lateran treaty of 1929.

Buying food in Rome: raw material for the Italian cuisine *left*. The rich variety of ingredients which characterizes Italian cuisine tends to bemuse the first-time shopper in the food markets. Business is brisk. Everyone knows exactly what to ask for. More impressively, the shopkeeper knows exactly where to find it. This store deals in a few of the dozens of types of cheeses and cold meats which are available.

Florence: the 'big white guy' *below*. Florentines call this statue in the Piazza della Signoria the 'big white guy' (Il Biancone). Officially he is Neptune, presiding over the fountain group which is dedicated to him. Though impressive in size, he is not among the best-proportioned or most successful of the statues in the Piazza. The sculptor Benvenuto Cellini clamored for the block of marble from which Neptune was sculpted but after some wrangling it was awarded to Bandinelli. However, most of the work was done after Bandinelli's death by Bartolomeo Ammannati (1511–92).

Rome. Early Christian Rome (where 11 of the 12 apostles were martyred) is represented by the Catacombs on the Via Appia, and by the tiny blackened churches like the Quo Vadis where Christ appeared and rebuked Peter as he fled from persecution.

Byzantine Rome and Rome of the Catholic Church are both evident, not only in St Peter's and the four patriarchal basilicas (all raised on the bones of saints), but in the amazing variety of primitive, Renaissance and Gothic arts still to be seen. Michelangelo's Pieta and the Sistine ceiling are supreme examples which should not be missed. Rome reflects every noble architectural period, from brick-and-tile Romanesque to florid marble and stucco baroque and the more recent imperialism of Mussolini. The monuments and statues, which are visible all over the modern city, make a lasting impression on the visitor. Secondary impressions are made by the marvelous fountain groups, the 2000-year-old aqueducts, the moods of the yellow Tiber and the calm serenity of the one real hill, the Janiculum behind Vatican City.

Just outside Rome are cool refuges from the heat, noise and expense of the city. Visit lizard-haunted Ostia Antica, the derelict classical port; the cascades of Tivoli; the villas of Frascati; the papal fortresses of the Alban hills; and the battlegrounds, ancient and modern, of Anzio.

Three hundred miles north of the capital, under the valleys and ski slopes of the Alps, lie the centers of Turin (industrial) and Milan (commercial). These are formidable cities of art and architecture – as, in their own ways, are the medieval showplaces of the Lombardy plain around them, such as Pavia, Parma, Mantua and Bologna. On the steeply terraced Ligurian coast lie the fashionable resorts of Portofino, Santa Margherita and Rapallo and the large port of Genoa, birthplace of Columbus and Paganini. Southward, rearing up from a pine-covered coastal plain, are the mountains of Carrara, suppliers of monumental marble to the world. Then comes Pisa and the Leaning Tower. The River Arno stretches back to Florence within a ring of vine- and cypress-covered hills. Under the Medici dynasty, from the 1400s

11

onwards, Florence became a shop-window of the arts, an emporium of paintings and sculptures, domes and towers by (among others) Giotto, Brunelleschi, Donatello, Ghirlandaio and Fra Angelico. Upstream, in the Valdarno and around the springs of the Tiber, was an extraordinary hotbed of genius. Michelangelo, Petrarch, Masaccio, Paolo Uccello, Sansovino, Vasari and Piero della Francesca were all born within a few miles of each other.

Old paths to Rome run by the stout walls of Siena, another proud medieval city, and by the Tiber valley to the painted tombs of the Etruscans. These tombs are chiefly around Tarquinia and Chiusi, and are bright memorials to the people who preceded the Romans and who were, by contrast, very easy-going. The Autostrada del Sole (Highway of the Sun) goes that way too. Italian highways, magnificently engineered, line the east and west coasts. The east-coast autostrada, the Adriatica, Venice to Brindisi, begins under the curved wall of the Alps in the region of Venetian villas. Within striking distance are the fantastic peaks of the Dolomites, the stately city of Trieste (least Italian of all Italian towns) and Padua, noted for learning and for Giotto's paintings. The Palladian villas of Vicenza and the Roman theater of Verona are also close by.

Venice has been called La Serenissima, Mistress of the Adriatic, Bride of the Sea.... The attractions here, which are as powerful as a magnet drawing in visitors, include dazzling music festivals and the romantic palaces on and around her waterways.

Florence: metropolis of Renaissance arts *right.* Seen from the hillslopes of Fiesole or Bellosguardo and from balcony viewpoints in the suburbs, the panorama of Florence is something, as the Italians say, to clutch the throat. Dominating all is Brunelleschi's terracotta cupola on the colored marble Duomo (cathedral) of Santa Maria del Fiore. Daring techniques were employed in building it and when new, in 1436, it was said to provide shade 'for all the inhabitants of Tuscany'. Giotto's 14th-century bell-tower, also in colored marble, rivals it for height. Visitors may ascend both Duomo (463 steps) and campanile (bell-tower) (414 steps) for views of the lovely Florentine hills.

Ponte Vecchio: oldest survivor of Arno bridges *left.* When the German army retreated through Florence in 1944 it destroyed every bridge but this one. The Ponte Vecchio has bridged the Arno for 600 years, yet it is younger than some of the shops which jut out from its parapets: they belonged to its predecessor.

Genoa: humble backwaters of La Superba *above.* Small compared with most great ocean terminals, the harbor of Genoa (called La Superba, 'the proud') is compact and well organized. In the creeks, medieval tenements prop each other up and lean toward the water's edge. It was in one of these waterfront slums that the greatest ocean traveler of them all was born: Christopher Columbus.

13

**Milan: the Duomo of a thousand
pinnacles** *above*. Milan's cathedral is
inferior in size only to those of Rome
and Seville (Spain). This modern
facade (completed 1890) lacks the
magic of the Duomo's older Gothic
features, which have inspired the
Milanese since the 14th century. An
elevator goes to the Duomo's upper
terrace, among the forest of spires,
but the underground canal, built to
transport the original building stone to
the foundations, is closed to traffic.

Southward, beyond the delta of the Po, Italy's longest river, stands
the inland seaport of Ravenna, with its Byzantine mosaics in churches
and mausoleums. Continuing south along the highway the republic of
San Marino, perched high in the mountains, can be glimpsed. The
highway then passes old fishing towns transformed into vacation-
lands. For every thousand tourists who visit Rimini, Pesaro and the
Abruzzi coastal resorts, scarcely five explore the hinterland; yet the
eastern slopes of the Apennines have much to offer, not least some
ancient walled towns with notable art collections.

The Gargano, the 'spur' on Italy's heel, and the offshore Tremiti
islands are developing fast under the impact of water sports – their
colored rocks, clear water, corals and submarine vegetation make
them exciting for sub-aqua swimmers.

The invisible frontier between Italy's faster, industrial north and her
slower rural south runs across the Gran Sasso d'Italia. Here, the

Sirmione: jewel of Italy's lakeland
right. The northern lakes — Maggiore, Garda, Como, Lugano and others — collect their waters from steep-sided Alpine valleys and distribute them to the Lombardy plain. Portrayed here is the baronial fortress of Scaliger ('della Scala') at Sirmione on Lake Garda. Protruding from the shore like the knobbled head of a club, it looks out on the 30-mile stretch of water.

Monte Pelmo: peak of the gleaming Dolomites *below.* Dolomite rock, with its porphyry (purple) slivers embedded in crystalline grey, comes from half a dozen sharp and spectacular massifs in north-eastern Italy — the last fling of the Alps before that great barrier slides into the Adriatic Sea. The Dolomites are geologically unique — of coral origin, it is said. This is Monte Pelmo (10,390 feet) from Colle Santa Lucia near the winter sports center of Cortina d'Ampezzo.

Apennines culminate in a 9000-foot plateau and the Abruzzi National Park, where bear and chamois roam. But distinctions are nowadays blurred. The teeming cities of Naples, Bari and Brindisi can hardly be called slow. Naples has her celebrated bay, ending in a promontory where renowned vacation centers like Amalfi, Positano, Sorrento and the island of Capri are wedged in a coastline of jagged inlets and headlands. Bari and Brindisi are big commercial ferry ports, the former having the Cathedral of Santa Claus (St Nicholas) on its waterfront, the latter with Roman monuments, a naval academy and a Greek flavor about its harbor. With the naval base of Taranto, they form a triangle enclosing the country of *trulli*, white stone-built beehive huts of prehistoric origin.

South of Naples and west of Taranto, the main routes follow the coastline. In the mountains, 5000 feet above, are the wildly beautiful valleys and rocks of Lucania and Calabria. On the shores citrus fruits grow, earning them romantic names such as Costa Viola and Jasmine Riviera. The old world's three major volcanoes can all be seen from here: Vesuvius, dormant; Stromboli in the Lipari islands, active; and Etna in Sicily, very active.

The ascent of 10,000-foot Etna, by bus and jeep from Catania, is a major tourist experience. You can walk on the crust, inches from the inferno, and also look out over the whole of Sicily. Traveling west through Sicily, a universally beautiful island, the highways penetrate poorer and more desolate country – though there is a blaze of Moorish flamboyance in Palermo and her mountain suburb of Monreale. In the far west, Trapani is the base for the tunny-fishing Egadi islands and for

Roman outpost in the Alpine foothills *right.* By the time it reaches Verona the River Adige has become a honey-colored flood, rolling under Ponte Scaligero. Barges glide with the current, their helmsmen dozing under green umbrellas. Verona comes into several Shakespearean plays and popular fancy has identified Juliet's house. The city is famous for its two Roman theaters – one among lawns and crumbling statuary where classical and Shakespearean drama is performed, the other a magnificent circular arena where, 50 years ago, the fashion in lavish *al fresco* opera was started.

'Siamo a tavola!' *left.* 'We are at the table!' – it means do not disturb, we're occupied for the next couple of hours. Love of family and food are Italian characteristics and Italians are never happier than when at a meal with relations and friends, preferably in the open air, with a little music to help things along. Farther south, forks are twirling and pasta is disappearing like snow in summer . . . but here the diners are in the Alto Adige or Sud Tirol (south of the Brenner Pass) and the menu has an Austrian flavor, with cooked ham, nuts, *pane tirolese* (almond bread) and the garnet-red wine of Lago di Caldaro.

Venice: stately waterway of La Serenissima *left.* In the heyday of her dignity, Venice was called La Serenissima, the 'most serene'. Attached to the mainland by a causeway, Venice consists mostly of canals, *rii* (branch canals), narrow walkways and bridges and the one large piazza of St Mark's. City life moves only by boat or on foot. The Grand Canal, sinuous main artery of Venice, shown here, is lined with more than 250 palaces and churches. The 'barbers' poles' (left foreground), striped with heraldic colors, were originally mooring posts for the palace gondoliers, who also wore their employers' colors.

The Bridge of Sighs *below.* Behind St Mark's basilica and at the back of the Doge of Venice's palace, this famous bridge connects ancient judgment hall with ancient prison. Hence its title: Ponte dei Sospiri (Bridge of Sighs).

Pantelleria, from which Tunisia is sometimes visible.

Italy is ringed with small islands. Among those which are visitable is Elba, an undulating extension of the Tuscan hill-country, with Napoleon's birthplace for an added attraction. Sardinia, rather neglected by mass tourism, is a large, unspoiled island of towering mountains, forests and lakes, where introverted little towns maintain strange and mysterious customs. In contrast, corners of the south-west and north of Sardinia have become the expensive playgrounds of the jet set.

TRAVEL TIPS

Italian winters can be bitterly cold, and spring and autumn rainy, but summers are long and hot. The tourist triangle of Florence, Rome and Venice grows congested in August – when, incidentally, nearly all Italy, including galleries and museums, shuts down for its own

Cefalù: new life for an old port *below.* Many Sicilian harbors look like this. The houses have sprouted as naturally as clumps of flowers. Fishing was their *raison d'être* and in tune with fishing's prosperity or depression they flourish or decline. Cefalù, on Sicily's northern coast, is lucky. Its beautiful situation under a promontory next door to a wide, curving bay has earned it smart hotels and the affection of many visitors.

Pompeii: a city brought back from the dead *right.* The cataclysmic eruption of Mount Vesuvius in 79 AD overwhelmed two elegant Roman cities on the Bay of Naples. Herculaneum, covered in lava, presented archeologists with problems but Pompeii, buried in ash, was easily excavated. Walking in its courts and villas we have the feeling that citizens may at any moment return and stare at us in astonishment. The picture shows the Greek god Apollo, minus his bow and arrow. This statue is a copy. Originals of many Pompeii figures and frescoes were removed to the National Museum of Naples.

vacation. Lovers of antiquities should linger in Rome, at Ostia Antica, Pompeii and Herculaneum, at the Etruscan tombs of Tarquinia and the beautiful Greek temples of Agrigento, Segesta and Syracuse in Sicily. The most scenic destinations are the Sorrentine peninsula, the Lombardy lakes and the riviera coastline east of Genoa. Development is highly geared towards tourists, but natural beauties abound almost everywhere, waiting for the enterprising traveler to discover them.

The country is not cheap to live or travel in, despite the weakness of the *lira.* It irks northern Europeans to have to pay to walk on the beach – though the fees collected do ensure that beaches are well kept.

Italian food is appreciated world-wide, so visitors know what to expect. The basic pasta, tomatoes and cheeses are reinforced with hosts of interesting vegetables, meats and fish. All regions, even some tiny townships, have their gastronomic specialties and the wines to go with them. It is proper, and cheaper, to eat and drink the produce of the locality and, when shopping for quality goods, to seek out the local specialty – silks of Como, glassware of Venice, leather of Florence, fashionwear of Milan and Rome.

Delphi: sacred hub of the classical world. High above the Gulf of Corinth, in a rocky hollow of Mount Parnassus, stands the hallowed sanctuary of Apollo. The rock-hewn theater and the treasuries and temples of his Sacred Way stand remote from the world. In classical mythology this spot was the navel of the earth, where man was linked with god.

GREECE

Athens · Delphi · Santorini
Mykonos · Crete · Meteora

There is a classic image of Greece: a blue sky, a blue sea, a milk-white classical column on a promontory, a scent of thyme in the still air. This picture springs to life in many Greek places, but the land is not all Hellenic temples, Corinthian pillars and marble amphitheaters. A rich variety of architecture spreads over the landscape. There are rock monasteries and massive forts from the Byzantine and Venetian eras, along with some startlingly modern city buildings and the unplanned harmony of the island towns. Greeks traveling abroad used to speak of 'going to Europe' – they did not regard themselves as members of that continent. Still rather remote from European influences, still near-eastern in outlook, Greece is by ordinary standards economically deprived. The barren, mountainous mainland and the broken-up geography make communications difficult. But the same features give mainland and islands striking panoramas and glamorous seascapes. If the Greeks could live on scenery they would be prosperous indeed.

A sharp-pointed mountain rises in the middle of Athens, identifying the city to mariners far out at sea. It is the Lycabettus (in modern Greek, Lykavitos) and it poses a problem for scholars: why is there no mention of this dominating landmark in the classical texts?

Whatever the reason, an early ascent by funicular railway is recommended for a survey of the city. At sunset you may see the purple haze which led Homer to describe Athens as 'violet-crowned'.

Other hills renowned in literature are prominent. There is Hymettus, noted for its honey, Parnes with its pine forests and Pentelico, the building-yard of snow-white marble for the ancient world. Closer, looking scarcely like a hill, is the most famous of all, the Acropolis, whose neolithic remains and Mycenean walls (1000 BC) support the Parthenon, temple of the city's virgin patroness, Athena. Close by the Parthenon is the Erechtheion with its pillars of sculpted maidens. Much rubble lies around, but laws against helping yourself to souvenir marble are strict.

The light is hard and bright, excellent for photography. You can see the Piraeus, the port of Athens, at the end of the boulevard two miles away. The hotels, night clubs and beaches of Glifada and Vouliagmeni stretch away towards the cliff-top temple of Poseidon at Cape Sounion. Westward is a tangle of isles among which the battle of Salamis was won against the Persian fleet in 480 BC.

Descending to central Athens, the city becomes fast-moving and garish, full of noise and people. Yet it is a fine place for strolling in.

The Parthenon: mainspring of golden-age creativity. Temples of ancient Greece, now weathered to cream color, were originally candy-striped. The Parthenon of Athens (440 BC), sanctuary of Athena, virgin goddess and protector of the city, must have looked garish by modern standards. But plain or colored it exemplifies the creative genius of Greece's golden age; the perfection of architectural elegance.

There are unexpected lofty columns and porticoes, toy Byzantine churches, the Hill of Muses where Socrates drank his hemlock and the Aeropagus where St Paul successfully attacked the pagan gods.

Westward from Athens, main roads and railways thread the Corinth isthmus, which is pierced by a ship canal. Corinth herself has been destroyed by earthquakes twice since 1858. This is not the 'golden Corinth' of antiquity, but a 100-mile-long gulf, leading out through narrows into the Ionian sea. It has been praised as the 'finest lake scenery in Europe'. We are now in the Peloponnese, the southern mainland of Greece, skirting hills where the Erymanthian boar roamed, where the Styx, river of Hades, flows and where Theseus had his adventure with the Procrustean bed. South of Patras, a ferry port for Italy, scented scrub country covers the plains of Elis where the Olympic Games were first held and where, every four years, the Olympic torch is kindled.

The arid mountains of the Peloponnese hide towns and sites of myth and legend, such as Mycenae with its Lion Gate and the supposed tombs of Agamemnon and his household. Sparta, once a

Hydra, steeped in maritime history *above.* This picturesque isle of the Saronic gulf attracts artists, historians and vacationists. Old naval cannon on the quay recall a stormy past. Hydra was heavily involved in the war of independence against the Turks. The trading fleets of Hydra's merchants (whose 19th-century mansions still stand) sailed all over the world. It was said that you might hear the Hydra dialect in any dockland from Cape Town to Buenos Aires.

powerful rival of Athens, is by contrast now undistinguished; and neighboring Arcadia, once associated by poets with rustic innocence, looks harsh and hostile. But the soft grey sands and blossoming tavernas of the Laconian gulf are beginning to attract foreign visitors.

North of Corinth's gulf, steep gorges are overgrown with olive trees which grow right to the sea's edge. Here stands Delphi, a major classical site. The treasuries, theater, temples and sanctuaries are easily accessible and extremely impressive. Delphi is most famous for the *omphalos* (navel of the world), where the oracle's enigmatic pronouncements decided the fates of nations and individuals. Among lasting memories of Delphi will be the pink, white and black *tholos* (round temple), the blue- and yellow-kerchiefed shepherd girls and the superb view seawards to the unruffled carpet of the Corinth gulf.

Black eagles, the birds of Zeus, can be seen whirling down from Parnassus, which soars behind Delphi to 8000 feet. Like Olympus farther north (9550 feet) the mountain is hard and dangerous to climb but winter sports are becoming popular on the lower slopes.

Under the cathedral arch at Santorini *above.* This Cycladean outpost has two names: Thira, the name of its principal town, and Santorini ('Saint Irene'), the name of its saint. It is an island turned inside out. The land surrounds the sea, ascending precipitously from a harbor 1300 feet deep. The harbor is the drowned crater of a volcano which blew its top around 1400 BC. Some say the catastrophe annihilated the Minoan civilization of Crete and inspired the myth of lost Atlantis. The Greek Orthodox priest on Santorini has a busy time looking after scores of tiny churches which sailors have built in gratitude for sanctuary from storms.

The Tholos: three columns of matchless beauty *left.* A short way downhill from the temple complexes of Delphi is the Tholos. The surviving Doric columns were restored this century by French archeologists after they had lain for 2000 years in the marshy woodland of the Castalian stream. Though incomplete, this is an exquisite piece of classical architecture, perfect in harmony and tranquillity. Nothing is known of its original function. The word *tholos* simply means 'rounded building'.

Mykonos: bright stopover on Aegean cruises *above.* Most Mediterranean cruise ships call at Mykonos, in the Cyclades, for those on board to see the windmills, sugar-cube dwellings, skeins of alleyways, narrow terraces and some of the 360 white-domed chapels. Other Cycladean islands have these features, but in the tourist imagination Mykonos has become the archetype. The harbor front is a bazaar of woven woollen goods, including the exclusive Mykonos belts.

Classical sites on the Delphi–Athens road include the Triple Way, where the fates led Oedipus to kill his father; and Thebes, where he unwittingly married his mother. On the Athens–Olympus–Thessaloniki route, through some rough country, hazardous in winter, you cross the plain of Marathon and the pass of Thermopylae, scenes of famous battles of antiquity (490 and 480 BC) between Greeks and Persians. Thermopylae means 'hot gates' and, like several coastal towns on the route, it has sulphur springs and offers spa treatment.

Greek islands are literally numberless: geographers cannot agree how many. The vacation favorites are Corfu and Zante, rich in botany and Venetian memories; Crete, a more savage land, popular with foreign tourists for its banana tree-fringed north coast and the fishing villages of the south; and Euboea, north-east from Athens, only a bridge away from the mainland. Euboea is most serene. It has sulphur springs, a few holiday villages and a scattering of classical ruins. It shares with the adjoining mainland a neat little inland sea and two spectacularly narrow shipping channels.

Between Greece and Turkey the Aegean Sea is littered with a kaleidoscope of islands. The ancients divided them into three groups: the Sporades ('strewn') in the north, the Cyclades ('circling') in the south and the Dodecanese ('twelve islands') in the east. People who know them all have their particular favorites: Skyros (grave of Rupert

Sounion's airy temple reflects the blue of sea and sky *below*. Cape Sounion rears a proud head at the southern tip of Attica, province of Athens. Sailors of 500 BC built this Doric temple to the sea-god Poseidon as an insurance against shipwreck. In certain lights the columns have an azure glow, as though from prolonged exposure to sea and sky. On this sacred headland Lord Byron's name is carved – he wrote that in all Greece he found no scene more fascinating than Cape Sounion. Under the promontory's west side there are hotels, restaurants and tourist pavilions, and the bathing is as good as anywhere in Greece.

The needlewoman: symbol of feminine virtue *right*. Since the time of Penelope, wife of Ulysses, women who toil at the loom and the needle in Mediterranean lands have been respected as models of virtue and patience. Nowadays it is the older generation of women, seated on rush-bottomed chairs just inside their doors or under the eaves at their thresholds, who do the knitting and embroidery; the regional dress of Crete, which includes a crocheted apron, is rarely seen. This Cretan woman is heiress to traditions of crochetwork and fabric weaving whose patterns and colors derive from decorations on Minoan tombs.

Crete: The Monastery of Arkadi *left.* The Monastery of Arkadi lies about 40 miles from the chief port of Herakleion. Following an abortive rising against the Turks in 1866, many Cretans were sheltered in its refectory. When the Turkish army broke in the abbot blew the place up, killing many defenders and even more attackers. The date of this decisive act, 7th November, has become Crete's national holiday.

The Meteora: six ecclesiastical penthouses *right.* Heading north-west through Thessaly towards the Pindus mountains, the road penetrates a gorge of astonishing natural curiosities. Even more astonishing is that 11th-century Byzantine monks, without mechanical aids, reached the tops of those monolithic pillars and built monasteries on them. Last century, all females – including hens and cats – were rigorously excluded. Only male visitors were received, pulled up in a basket. Lord Curzon asked how often a new rope was provided and was told: 'When the old rope breaks'. Of 24 monasteries, only six survive. But they now have stairways – and nuns.

St. Chrysostomos, Sifnos *below.* This enchanting building is typical of the bright white little churches built in the same style for centuries and seen all over the Greek islands. St. Chrysostomos dates from the mid-18th century.

Brooke, an English poet), Skiathos and Skopelos in the north; Delos (sacred hub of the Cyclades), Thira (a ring of sheer cliffs which surround a sea-filled volcanic crater) and Mykonos (noted for windmills and chapels) in the Cyclades. The largest and most historic of the Dodecanese group is Rhodes. Other warm favorites include Kos, where Hippocrates, the 'father of medicine', was born; Patmos, where a huge monastery embraces St John's cave of the Apocalypse (where the Book of Revelations was written); and Kalimnos, home of sponge-divers. Scores of islands like them, all with their spartan quayside cafés, ouzo-drinkers passionately discussing politics, bouzoukis twanging nearby, and the aromatic thyme-scents drifting in, have become the secret hideaways of discerning travelers.

TRAVEL TIPS

Contrary to widely held beliefs, the Greeks are friendly, outgoing and generous. How long that will last is another question – in tourist areas a certain cynicism is evident, brought on by the uncouth (in Greek eyes) behavior of foreigners. There are, however, immense cultural differences between regions. The Epirot of the north-west is a foreigner in Athens. Mainlanders and islanders are poles apart. Cretans, Rhodians and Corfiots have a life and character all their own.

Bus travel is very cheap, Aegean cruises (from the Piraeus) of one to seven days are exceptionally good value, car rental is moderately expensive. There are many official holidays and little business is done in the afternoons, though shops may open again in the evenings. There is scarcely a public lavatory in the whole country.

In the steps of the Master. To stand
where their Lord and his disciples
stood has been the dream of
Christian believers down the ages.
Today it is an easy journey to the
ancient rabbinical town of Tiberius. A
modern holiday resort and doorstep
to the Sea of Galilee, Tiberius is rich
in biblical associations.

ISRAEL
Jerusalem · Tiberius · Jericho

Israel is a small country – about the size of Connecticut, if we ignore the territories occupied in 1967. Much of the land consists of barren hills and stony desert, awesome in their desolation. The principal river, the Jordan, is a mere trickle. But for those who follow in the steps of the prophets or trace the wanderings of Christ and his disciples every square yard is precious, every scene a page from a biblical text, or from the Koran. Jerusalem, which means so much to Jews and Christians, is also a holy city of Islam.

Pilgrims have always flocked to Israel and nowadays tourists follow them. Superficial impressions can be misleading, for it turns out that the lonely hills conceal delightful valleys, bursting with oranges, grapefruit and other exotic fruits and vegetables. To compensate for lack of rivers, Israel has four seas (Mediterranean, Red, Galilee and Dead), all with excellent bathing and boating. The contrast of patriarchal and ultra-modern – as though the society took 20 centuries in one leap – is continually astonishing.

'Next year in Jerusalem' – the prayer of exiled Jews down the ages is echoed by thousands of prospective tourists. The idea of Jerusalem the Golden is shared by all. Perhaps it is the deep-rooted spiritual response; perhaps the fact that Jerusalem is always in the news.

Despite the turmoil of the centuries the city is an amazingly attractive one. The old proverb is often quoted: 'God gave the world ten bushels of beauty, of which nine fell on Jerusalem'. Like many famous cities it is built on hills – but these are genuine hills and the towers and cupolas, low pantiled Byzantine domes and flat-roofed houses shine out from their crests. Main streets are always crowded and among the jeans and t-shirts, the working overalls and berets, is the somber garb of those who cling to traditional Jewish dress. Most shops and stalls have a countrified air and there is a surprising absence of big banks and offices, department stores and concert halls. (They are found in the new town of Tel Aviv, 40 miles away.)

Inside the dark walls of the Old City, with their eight fortress-like gates, stands the church of the Holy Sepulchre, built on the spot where, according to tradition, Christ was buried and rose again. Here, and in the adjoining Christian quarter, are numerous sites associated with Christ's trial and execution, the *via dolorosa* and Garden of Gethsemane among them.

The holy places of the Moslems close by are the ornate mosques of Aksa and Omar. From the site of Omar (Dome of the Rock), say the

Jerusalem, where prayers ascend to God. At the Western Wall, popularly called the Wailing Wall, the Jewish God is always present. The wall is the last surviving fragment of the temple which the Romans destroyed in AD 70. Prayer-notes and small keepsakes are deposited in crevices between the stones, to be recovered when the exiled owners return to Jerusalem. The golden cupola is the Dome of the Rock, actually a mosque, and to the left is the silver-domed mosque of Aksa.

Moslems, the prophet Mahomet ascended to heaven. Jews believe that on this spot, where the Temple once stood, the patriarch Abraham offered his son Isaac for sacrifice.

Sights in Old Jerusalem which are not to be missed are the Wailing Wall (properly the Western Wall) and the Damascus Gate, near which the Arabs have their markets and craft shops, like an Oriental bazaar. The most eye-catching of New Jerusalem's buildings are the four-square, flat-roofed Knesset (the Israeli parliament building), the bottle-shaped Shrine of the Book, and the Hebrew university. An interesting feature, with good views of the New Town, is the Billy Rose Art Garden, which is furnished with monumental open-air sculptures.

As a meeting place of routes in biblical Palestine, this city is an obvious touring center. Place names from both Old and New Testaments are virtually all that survive to remind us of the ancient events. Many people fulfill a lifelong ambition by standing in mountainous Hebron, the royal city of Canaan, known to have been visited by Abraham. Pilgrims make the fatiguing 250-mile journey across the desert to see Mount Sinai (8537 feet) where Moses received the Commandments.

The New Testament sites are easier to cover. Bethlehem, birthplace of Christ, is 20 minutes in a taxi from central Jerusalem. The circuit of Nazareth (where Christ's parents lived), Cana (first miracle), Capernaum and Bethsaida on the Sea of Galilee (where Christ gathered his apostles and preached and healed the sick), and back to Jerusalem via the Jordan valley and Jericho is comfortably accomplished in a day. Elaborate churches mark the major historical sites, and places like Masada, revered in Jewish history, are also on this route.

Apart from Jerusalem, several cities merit attention. It is a fine scenic excursion by road or rail from Jerusalem to Haifa, through the plain of Sharon, the Roman ruins of Cesarea and the gap between Mount Carmel and the sea. Haifa's old town sprawls picturesquely round its bay and its modern suburbs climb the slopes of Mount Carmel. The summit is accessible by underground railway and from its upper station a skyline drive goes along the crests of the hills, with the Lebanon and the hills of Galilee in view. Israel's major port, Haifa

Patience and piety at the Wailing Wall *above.* This quiet figure wears the black ankle-length frock-coat, broad-brimmed velvet hat and sidelocks of the orthodox Oriental Jew. Many such Jews live in the Mea Sherim quarter of the city where rabbis and divinity students study the laws and prophecies. Jewish festivals include the Day of Atonement when the whole family fasts and prays. On the eve of the Passover the Exodus story is read and they eat the Passover meal of bitter herbs and unleavened bread.

Onion domes reflect a Tsar's filial piety *far right.* Scores of Jewish and Moslem sects and representatives of all the Christian faiths have built their houses of worship in Jerusalem. This is a Russian Orthodox church near the Garden of Gethsemane. It is one of the churches which Tsar Alexander III (reigned 1881–94) built to honor the memory of his mother.

Jerusalem: surrealist casket for a precious scroll *right.* Not a visitor from outer space but a remarkable piece of modern architecture: the Shrine of the Book. It is part of the Israel Museum opposite the Knesset (parliament house). Here the famous Dead Sea scrolls are kept. The biblical and sectarian texts, some from around 100 BC, written on parchment, wrapped in linen and enclosed in storage pots, were found by two Arab shepherd boys at Qumran on the Dead Sea in 1947.

can also claim to be the nation's cultural capital, with its own symphony orchestra, several big concert halls and theaters, galleries and museums.

Akko (formerly Acre), on the edge of Haifa's bay, is the old Crusader port. It is a startling mixture of crumbling Saracen walls and smart new apartment blocks and factories.

Most round-Israel tours end at Tel Aviv because it is close to the international airport at Lod (ancient Lydda). This is a brand-new city, rapidly growing, with more than half a million inhabitants. Tel Aviv has the big national institutions, the state museums and head offices of business houses, as well as plenty of theaters, shops and street cafés. English soldiers and statesmen connected with Palestine's development earlier this century are still commemorated. The main street is Allenby Street and the seafront walk is the Herbert Samuel Esplanade.

For a touch of the quaint and artistic, Tel Aviv is complemented by Jaffa. Now a suburb of Tel Aviv, it is a well-restored old community with many archaic features adapted to present-day needs – and, of course, orange plantations.

The Sea of Galilee, well below sea-level, and the Dead Sea, lower still – the lowest place on earth – offer bathing. Non-swimmers are perfectly safe because the high level of salt makes them unusually buoyant. (You must pay to use the beaches.) The Negev desert and its ruined 2000-year-old city of Avdat are impressively silent. South of the Negev the new town of Eilat is a flourishing winter resort on the Red Sea hemmed in by savage scenery. Finally, and not least, the Israeli 'economic miracle' – the assimilation of a tremendous influx of population since 1948, the cultivation of crops and fruit orchards and

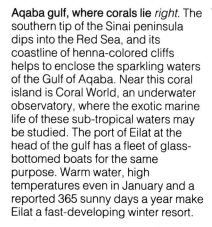

Aqaba gulf, where corals lie *right*. The southern tip of the Sinai peninsula dips into the Red Sea, and its coastline of henna-colored cliffs helps to enclose the sparkling waters of the Gulf of Aqaba. Near this coral island is Coral World, an underwater observatory, where the exotic marine life of these sub-tropical waters may be studied. The port of Eilat at the head of the gulf has a fleet of glass-bottomed boats for the same purpose. Warm water, high temperatures even in January and a reported 365 sunny days a year make Eilat a fast-developing winter resort.

Jerusalem: inside the Old City *left*. Eight gates in a ring of crenellated brownstone walls give access to the multiracial communities of the Old City. Names of gates are evocative of old highways: Jaffa Gate, Damascus Gate. Another is the Lions' Gate – it has stone lions carved beside it. A fourth is the Dung Gate where citizens deposited their garbage. Inside, on all-pedestrian streets and alleyways, men and donkeys go about their business and tourists bargain for religious souvenirs, miscellaneous trinkets and, here and there, a genuine item of art or craftwork.

Arab shepherd comes to market *far right*. The hard life of the shepherd, which Aristophanes recommended as a suitable punishment for disobedient slaves, is rarely harder than in the arid Sinai and Negev deserts and among the sparse scrub of what, in Israel, are called pastures. This shepherd, bargaining in an Israeli market, is Arab – which sometimes makes life harder.

the raising of cattle and poultry where such activities were thought impossible – is a spectacle to arouse the wonder and admiration of all visitors.

TRAVEL TIPS

Polite foreigners take a little time to adjust to the Israeli philosophy of behavior. Standing in line is unknown: at every bus-stop or ticket barrier you must join a ruthless stampede. City streets are racetracks and pedestrians must keep their wits about them. In every walk of life Israelis are go-getters and the sooner the visitor adopts their ways the sooner he or she will feel at home. It is a workable system as long as everyone conforms to it.

The Israelis welcome tourists – and their currency – and are proud and happy to show the remarkable achievements of a society which started with little and has accomplished much. For peace and quiet and an easy-paced life you must go among the poorer Arabs or the Bedouins of Beersheba and the Negev. Israelis work long hours and are inclined to be impatient with time-wasting idlers.

Bus transport is efficient, but only Jerusalem and the coastal towns have railways. Signs are in English and Hebrew, English being the *lingua franca* of a polyglot population. Food is cosmopolitan. Traditional Jewish dishes are readily available and most hotels observe old prohibitions which forbid pork and meals containing both meat and milk – that is, if you order steak you forfeit the cream in your coffee. Sabbath closing (late Friday to late Saturday) is strictly

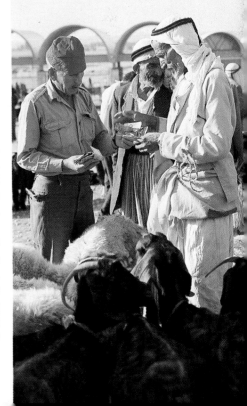

On the road of the Good Samaritan
above. Standing on the road to Jericho is the Greek Orthodox monastery of St George. Barely a century old, it stands on very ancient foundations – as do some other monasteries along this road where the parable of the Good Samaritan is set. In its early days this monastery housed hundreds of monks, nowadays there are only a few.

Masada: an act of determined self-sacrifice *right.* Masada was King Herod's prestige palace, an impregnable stronghold overlooking the Dead Sea. After years of Jewish struggles against Roman rule had culminated in the destruction of Jerusalem in 70 AD, 1000 rebels – men, women and children – occupied Masada. Three years passed and they faced surrender or suicide. They chose the last and hurled themselves from the ramparts. The event has passed into Jewish history as an unforgettable example of lives laid down in the defence of freedom.

enforced in some places, not so strictly in others; offices, shops and banks tend to close and the only public transport is taxis. Some cafés and restaurants close and in hotel dining rooms, which remain open, visitors may be asked not to smoke. Israel is a costly country for the tourist – tipping is endemic, 15%–18% expected. But it is generally well worth it.

The pyramid of Cheops: an expression of Pharaonic might. Set on the ridge between Nile and Western Desert, visible from Cairo's minarets, the pyramids at Giza are the most dramatic symbols of royal power and technological brilliance. The largest, the pyramid of Cheops, is 450 feet high.

EGYPT

Cairo . Giza . Minya
Luxor . Thebes . Edfu
Abu Simbel . Alexandria

The relief map of Egypt presents an extraordinary picture. One green, wavering strip tapers from north to south (the Nile valley), and a bunch of greenery sprouts at its head (the Nile delta). All the rest is brown and empty, except for here and there a rock summit or a disappointed watercourse. Egypt is the land of really ancient history, twice as old as that of Greece or Rome. When the Jews began their history, Egypt's was already on the wane. But the brilliant civilization of this nation, which remained peacefully introverted and did not go in for foreign adventures, is also brilliantly documented, both in living monuments on the ground and in the researches of archeologists.

The Pyramids of Giza and the Sphinx have been for centuries a major focus of foreign travel. Nearer our own times, scholars and excavators have located and uncovered the splendor and majesty of equally staggering relics at Memphis, Beni Hassan, Abydos, Thebes, Karnak, Abu Simbel and other sites along the upper Nile. Culturally speaking, Egypt is the country to which we graduate after completing our courses in the heritage of Greece and Rome.

Cairo is an ancient city, possibly the oldest town in Egypt, possibly contemporary with the Giza pyramids (2500 BC) which are just across the river. Its early name, Misr, is now the Arab name for Egypt. As with Rome and Athens, Cairo's story is told in her everyday streets as well as in her fine museums. There are reminders of the caliphs (seventh century AD), of Saladin (12th century) and of the Ottoman sultans (16th century). Many a medieval *suq* (bazaar) survives and the domes of graceful old mosques stand out above the sprawl of European-style shops, gardens and high-rise buildings which began to change the appearance of the metropolis during the economic boom following the opening of the Suez Canal in 1869.

Liberation Square, a spacious geometrical layout of greenery and fountains, is the heart of Cairo, the point of departure for tours of the mosques and museums. These are conceived on a generous scale, with Oriental extravagance. It is better to linger and savour the atmosphere of a few, rather than attempt a comprehensive round-up of the many. Among city mosques, El-Azhar (built 972 AD, much elaborated later) and the Mohammed el-Nasir (1304) reveal the Arabs' skill with color and intricate design, lavish but tasteful. Arabesques (stylized paintings of Koranic texts) are prominent. The blue tiles of

Cairo: a view of the citadel. Cairo's 'modern' history began after the Arab conquest in 641 AD when the caliphs started improving a collection of mud huts on the east bank of the Nile. Under Saracen and Turk the city knew many changes, but still it grew. Now it is the largest city in Africa and in the Islamic world. The 12th-century citadel, pictured here, will be a major historical attraction when its restoration is completed. The mosque was begun in 1824 by the bloodthirsty pasha Mohammed Ali, and is locally known as the Alabaster Mosque.

45

The art of the belly-dancer *left*. The Egyptian belly-dancer, clothed or unclothed, perpetuates one of the oldest entertainment traditions of the Middle East. Performers are selected and trained for the job from an early age and they enjoy the prestige and acclaim of rock stars. Not every girl is physically equipped for it, but Egyptians seem to be and the gyrations and contortions of the experts are unbelievable. But belly-dancing for tourist consumption is a pale imitation of belly-dancing in the traditional mode at private clubs and houses.

the Aq-Sunqur or 'Blue' mosque deserve detailed inspection. Among museums, the most important is the huge Egyptian museum on Liberation Square, where Tutankhamen's golden mask and treasures from his tomb are displayed.

The major sights of Cairo are on the right (east) bank of the Nile. To go to the west bank you may cross the island called Gezira, where exhibition grounds, golf course and athletic clubs are situated. Also here are the plush residential section, and the fretted Cairo Tower (614 feet) rather like a stretched-out pineapple, with restaurant and observation platform.

The Cairo citadel, a typical Saracenic palace-fortress complex built by Saladin around 1200 AD, offers another panoramic view of the city from its towers. Here too are the Abdin (presidential) palace, airy and dignified, the Ezbekiya gardens with rare tropical plants, and the Nile Corniche, a riverside drive with all the smart stores

Fruit-seller of Cairo *left*. Sticky dates, prickly pear, guava, pomegranates and nuts are the produce of a land which displays much broad-leaved vegetation but few orchards. The fruit-seller is a member of the *fellahin*, the peasant class which forms 96% of the population. These humble folk are the descendants of the Nile valley's ancient inhabitants who carved the splendid statuary and built the temples, tombs and pyramids.

Silent watchers on the Nile *above*. On the upper Nile at Luxor stands the 3400-year-old 'temple of palaces'. Two miles downstream is Karnak with its even older and bigger Great Temple of Amun. Between the exit from one temple and the entrance to the other, were sacred processional routes. They are now known as the Avenues of Sphinxes. Our picture shows one of them. Allow plenty of time for visits to the Luxor–Karnak area.

along it (prices here are fixed, unlike those in the bazaars).

The one stupendous excursion from Cairo, which can last days or weeks or years, is the trip up the Nile. The overwhelming majority of Egyptians are born, live, work and die on the banks of this river, which is the world's longest. Going upstream, only six miles from Cairo, the Pyramids of Giza, the Sphinx and five other groups of smaller pyramids are first seen, strung along 25 miles of the river's west bank. The Giza pyramids were built around 4500 years ago to house the mortal remains of successive Pharaohs. Their heights range from 200 to 450 feet and it requires stamina to climb them. Each ridge of stone is more than three feet high. Dwarfed by the Great Pyramid, yet a massive object itself (240 feet long, 65 feet high), the antique Sphinx presents a human face on a lion's body. It is badly weathered but still a marvel of enigmatic grandeur. All these constructions are floodlit at night and visible from Cairo.

Immediately south of Cairo are the ruins of once-mighty Memphis, shrouded in palm trees, and the necropolis and stepped pyramid of Saqqara, an important archeological site.

Heading upstream, it is only the time available and the mode of transport – train, automobile or river steamer – which dictate what to see. A lifetime would scarcely be long enough for all the ancient temples, pylons (gateways), obelisks and statues which are massed along the steep, orange-colored slopes of the valley. Many, which would be precious heirlooms in another country, must be passed by

Sky-pointing landmark of Karnak *below*. No single architectural novelty so fascinated the Europeans in Egypt as the obelisk (it means 'needle' or 'sharp instrument'). This one, at the fourth pylon (gatehouse) of the Great Temple of Amun (Karnak), is the tallest and heaviest (97 feet, 320 tons) of those which remain in their original sites. Only the Lateran obelisk in Rome (101 feet) exceeds it in height.

In the Valley of the Kings *right*. Across the Nile from Karnak and Luxor (no bridge, but regular ferry services), on raised ground above the flood level of the river, is the necropolis (burial ground) of Thebes. Tracks lead westward for a mile or so towards important groups of temples and tombs which date from the Middle Kingdom (2000 BC) and the New Kingdom (1400 BC). This is the Valley of the Kings. The most famous tomb of all is that of Tutankhamen (died 1339 BC). Its discovery in 1922 was the archeological sensation of modern times.

with a single glance. In the neighborhood of Luxor is the densest concentration of vast and delicately sculpted temples (at Karnak), death chambers and painted tombs (at Thebes) and the famous Valley of the Kings. Most visitors arrive at Luxor by air: it is 470 miles from Cairo.

Temples and tombs of ornate splendor continue to line the course of the Nile to Aswan, 690 miles from Cairo, with its Old and New Cataract hotels overlooking riverscapes of red rocks, bunched palm groves and white-sailed feluccas. Aswan is the starting-point for a five-hour air excursion to the farther shores of artificial Lake Nasser and the colossal statuary of Abu Simbel, regarded by some as the most impressive of all the monuments of antiquity. The civil engineers of six nations co-operated to lift the statutes from their original site, now deep under the lake.

Although the attractions of the Nile can dominate a visit to Egypt, there are other places which will not disappoint the enterprising traveler. These include the coral strands of the Red Sea, the Suez

Edfu: sacred symbol of the sun-god
right. Horus the sun-god, offspring of Isis and Osiris, was the first deity to be acknowledged and worshipped in all the temples of Egypt. Early kings regarded themselves as his reincarnation. Horus came to be represented by a solar disc with wings, but at first his symbol was the falcon. These two black granite birds stand guard at the entrance to his temple at Edfu – the most perfect of Nile temples, with its bas-reliefs still sharply incised.

The cult of royal death *left*. Serious and complicated ritual attended the deaths of Egypt's kings and queens. Mummification and the establishment of impressive houses for the dead made costly and time-consuming demands on the Egyptian economy. The royal tombs of Thebes were mini-palaces, loaded with treasure. Among them is this mausoleum – never completed – of an unknown king. The mummified body, suitably adorned, was laid to rest and sealed up in a weighty stone sarcophagus.

Canal and garden town of Ismailia, the raffish, disorganized seaport of Port Said and the mosques, cathedrals and fortresses of European-style Alexandria.

TRAVEL TIPS

Temperatures in winter reach the 20sC (70sF), in summer they hover round the mid-30sC (100sF). November to March is, therefore, the best season for travel. Nights can be cold all year round. Public transport is cheap but always crowded and uncomfortable – but this does not apply to the sleeper-diner trains on the Cairo–Luxor–Aswan route, which are designed for tourists (early booking of seats is imperative), or the passenger boats on the Nile, which travel between Luxor and Aswan and less frequently between Luxor and Cairo. Complicated documentation, the closing of country roads at night and traffic signs only in Arabic make private motoring an ordeal. It is best on a first visit to join and stay with an organized tour. Beggars are everywhere. Violence against tourists is very rare.

Whether independent or 'packaged', visitors to Egypt should not

drink tap water, nor expect to find hotels outside Cairo, Luxor, Aswan and Alexandria. They must also respect local customs and should not dress provocatively, criticize the regime or the religion, go shopping on Fridays (the Moslem holiday), or enter mosques with shoes on. Customers are expected to haggle over prices, although this is a mere formality since things are cheap enough.

The big city hotels, where 99% of tourists stay, offer an international cuisine with good lamb-based dishes. Most restaurants provide only the Arab diet of highly spiced meats and ultra-sweet pastries. Coffee is excellent and a few well-known brands of soft drinks and mineral waters are widely available in tourist centers. Egyptians are forbidden to drink wines, but they make them for export and the larger hotels serve quite drinkable whites (mostly sweet) and reds (usually dry). Less sophisticated restaurants and inns will not serve alcohol even to non-Moslems.

Colossal god-kings rescued from drowning *left.* Human figures alongside convey no true impression of the stupendous scale of these memorials to a king's megalomania (Rameses II, 1290 BC, declared he was a god). The place was Abu Simbel. In 1960 the name made headlines: the new Aswan dam, creating a 200-mile-long reservoir, would have submerged the temple complex to a depth of 150 feet. Through Unesco an international engineering consortium lifted the antiquities and re-erected them on higher ground. The job took six years and cost 50 million dollars.

Alexandria: halfway house to the Orient *below.* Created by Alexander the Great (331 BC), Alexandria suffered loss of status when the Suez Canal was opened and the harbor at the Nile mouth ceased to be a principal port. It still has its old forts, dotted along the waterfront, but now it is a thriving cotton port. Pictured here is Fort Qaitbay, now a naval museum, built on the site of Pharos, the famous lighthouse of antiquity.

NORTH AFRICA

Morocco • Tunisia

Stately pageant of the camels.
Invisible under wraps, the camel riders are as statuesque as minarets as they journey through the streets of a Moroccan town.

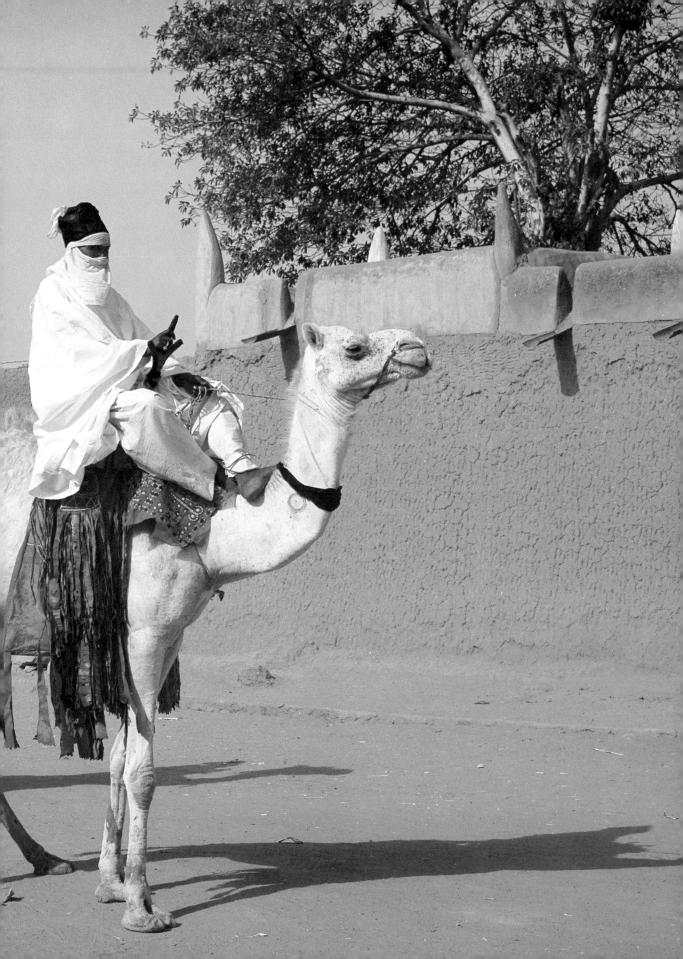

Approaching North Africa by sea or air, your first thought may be that you made a bad mistake. What kind of travel experience can these low, featureless shores, these empty wastes offer? On closer inspection, the low sand-dunes are high mountains and the desert contains greenery. Colors range from grey to orange and pale yellow to deep crimson in rocky outcrops which wind and sand have sculpted into surrealist shapes. On the ground, the visitor finds palm-lined boulevards, streets of woody vines, French or Spanish colonial mansions, Moorish palaces, and even Roman pillars. Tunisia's great attraction is her 800-mile-long ribbon of white sand, tracing the indentations of her coastline on the Mediterranean sea. Morocco comprises a variety of scenic landscapes, from the towering High Atlas and the romantic Rif to rich dales of oaks, cedars and olives; and, by contrast, the glamor of towns like Tangier, Fez, Marrakesh and the capital, Rabat. Tourism in both Tunisia and Morocco also offers the thrill of a sortie into the desert, the untamed Sahara.

Several nations – Romans, Byzantines, Turks, Spaniards and French – had a hand in the building of Tunis. Much of the stone came from the obliterated city of nearby Carthage. Modern Tunis's most striking features, the Hilton and high-rise Africa hotels, were also contributed by foreign entrepreneurs, and the capital city of Tunisia is therefore a striking blend of different cultures.

The main street, like all Tunisian main streets since 1956, is Avenue Bourguiba – name of the president who since that date has been bringing feudal Tunisia into the 20th century. A causeway takes trains and automobiles across the 'lake' of Tunis (more of a lagoon) to the sandy beaches of satellite towns. La Goulette and Carthage on the left and Hammam Lif on the right constitute 'Tunis-by-the-sea'.

The city has a respectable number of mosques, churches and museums, a citadel, and parks full of luxuriant shrubs. One of the most fascinating sights for strangers is the medina. Meaning simply 'town' in Arabic, the word is applied to the Arab market quarter of North African towns. The medina of Tunis is a warren of *suqs* (bazaars), meandering through covered passages, scented with the promise of an Arabian night's adventure. What with the perfume suq, the spice and wool-dyers' *suq* and other aromatic *suqs*, the confusion of odors in the confined space is hard to take at first. Yet this is one of the best-run and most hygienic of North African medinas.

Bijou apartments for nomads – and tourists. Tired of being nomads, a 12th-century Berber tribe flocked into Medinine and other villages of Tunisia's deep south. They built for themselves *ghorfas* (chambers), tiered caverns of rock and mud, up to six stories high. Holes in ceilings linked one with another. The upper tiers have now collapsed, but the lower are used for stores and a few are still inhabited – with television, refrigerators and piped water inside them. Around Ghoumrassen, 25 miles south of Medinine, tourists who believe in trying everything once may sign up for a *ghorfa* bed and breakfast.

Carthage is now a residential suburb. The extensive but much-knocked-about ruins of the ancient city, which figured so much in classical history, have been collected into its well-laid-out museums.

Much of coastal Tunisia merits leisurely inspection. It is a pleasant trip to Cape Bon (1000 feet), the nearest point to Europe, past sleepy lagoons and across rough ridges. Going south, do not omit Hammamet, the most sophisticated resort in the country, with magnificent parkland and beaches; nor the new mosque (a gift from native-born President Bourguiba) and old *ribat* (part monastery, part barracks) in Monastir, a center for fishing, yachting and sea-bathing; or Gabes farther south, an old Roman town next door to a lovely oasis which follows a watercourse right into the sea, twisting and turning in the ravines; or Djerba, across the bay from Gabes, a serene spot to which emperors and caliphs retired for relaxation.

From Gabes it is 130 miles by road and desert track to the fringes of

Monastir, a presidential birthplace
below. Two decorative cupolas epitomize the grace of Moorish architecture. The town is Monastir, birthplace of Tunisia's president. On the coast road 75 miles south of Tunis, it was the seaside resort where Tunisia's tourist industry first flourished.

Tunis Cathedral: the colonial-ecclesiastical style *right*. A French saint, Vincent de Paul, canonized for his success in buying Christian captives from Barbary pirates, gave his name to this Roman Catholic cathedral. It stands in Place de l'Indépendance at the end of the main street, Avenue Bourguiba, named after the President. Other street-names of Tunis are apportioned between French and Arab personalities: Jean Jaurès, Charles de Gaulle, Ibn Haldoun, Gamal Abdel Nasser. There is also an Avenue Franklin.

the Sahara and the oasis-villages of the Jerid, charming arrangements of sand-bricked cottages, minarets and colonnades picked out in geometrical patterns of reds and yellows.

Cross the 12-mile-wide Straits of Gibraltar from Europe to Morocco and you feel you are still in Andalusian Spain. But old rambling Tangier provides a foretaste of the Moorish magic for which foreign visitors clamor. On the road south, through the green, well-watered Atlantic coastlands where the beaches are inviting but the ocean is often turbulent, the first big town is Rabat. Its port developed by Spaniards, Rabat has something of a Spanish atmosphere. But the old city, confined within a girdle of pink latticed walls, contains authentic Islamic buildings. Beyond the frowning 17th-century *kasbah* gate and the Andalusian gardens inside it, an old regime, older than Spain, displays its arms, tapestries and precious stones. In the adjacent medina (market) the baffling corridors packed with merchants and

Tunis: ceramic tiles frame an old medina *left.* Lavishly tiled portals look out from a Moorish terrace on the roofs and covered *suqs* (bazaars) of the fortified inner city. This town-within-a-town is an amazing labyrinth where every dark passage seems to end in a locked door. A street-plan is available – and essential – for tracing the *suqs* of the perfumes, the cloths, the silks, the spices, the knitted hats, the weapons, the various metals . . . and the slave market, which functioned until this century. Box-like above the rooftops, the Great (or Olive-tree) Mosque (begun 8th century, finished 18th century) thrusts out its tower (left of picture).

Djerba, the isle of Calypso *right.* Calypso's isle or the lotus-eaters' isle? – one way or another, tourist propaganda is determined to get Djerba into the Odyssey. Certainly it has a mythological air, though there may soon be more hotels than palm-trees. Square-shaped with sides about 14 miles long, Djerba in the Gulf of Gabes has a short ferry and a long causeway to the mainland. In the markets of the capital Houmt Souk (7000 inhabitants), arts and crafts reign supreme. The island is famous for pottery, silks, woollens, leatherwork, silver, woven carpets, and sponges.

craft-workers wind away into impenetrable mazes. On Friday mornings, at nearby Bab Zaer, the royal palace, spectators gather to see the King ride in procession to the Great Mosque, attended with tremendous pomp and ceremony.

Casablanca, originally a small trading post, grew to be Morocco's largest city when another colonial power, France, chose it as a military base and seaport for its communications with the interior. It is now a city with plenty of traffic and night-life, architecturally a cross between modern European and ancient Moorish, with an extensive (but steadily diminishing) ring of shanty-town suburbs.

Trade from the Sahara was channeled into Casablanca through Fez (170 miles away) and Marrakesh (150 miles). These two cities offer the real unadulterated Morocco. The journey to Fez via Meknes (itself a tourist town, with gaunt Berber ruins) takes in fertile valleys and a varied plant and tree life. Fez is magnificently situated, with well-kept monuments of Moroccan history dating back to the ninth century AD. Its medina has the dubious distinction of being the most labyrinthine in North Africa – its myriad colors and smells are bewildering too. Visitors spend days getting lost there.

Fez looks to the Atlantic, Marrakesh to the desert. Marrakesh is renowned for shaded walks and parks: a city built within an oasis, where space for courts and mosques and forts on a grand scale has been found. It has the country's tallest minarets, biggest theological

Tozeur: a walk to the Paradise Garden *above.* Signs say To The Oasis – and the motor road, over a salty depression notorious for mirages, is quite exciting. Then Tozeur looms up: not a mirage. It has villas, a grubby medina, a railway station and an airstrip. The oasis adjoins the town. You can stroll to it. Huge date-palms, many pools and springs, a Paradise Garden with rose-arbors, soft-fruit orchards and a holy jujube tree . . . it is fresh and cool, it is magnificent, but it is not quite Rudolf Valentino.

61

colleges, most extensive medina . . . and its principal square, Djemaa-el-Ena, turns at nightfall into North Africa's most glittering fairground.

Good mountain roads climb through the Rif, from both Fez and Tangier, to Oujda on the Algerian frontier 200 miles away. These routes are delightfully scenic. Their rich, glossy green vales, vineyards, orchards and forests of pine and cedar with abundant water and wildlife, dispose once and for all of the myth that North Africa is mostly sand, snakes and scorpions.

TRAVEL TIPS

Both Tunisia and Morocco are progressive lands, currently in transition between the stern Islamic heritage and more modern European ideas. Touches left over from French and Spanish colonial traditions add variety to the ways of life. Tunisians and Moroccans are proud and polite people with formal manners and a slightly disapproving (though ever tolerant) attitude to foreign foibles. Spring and early summer are the best months for touring. Shopping is a delight, especially in the medinas, and prices are reasonable for carpets, lace, silks, leather, jewelry, metalwork and certain antiques. European-style restaurants are making headway in larger towns, the menus of the new grand hotels are ambitious and still quite cheap, and extreme care is taken over the 'chef's special'. In smaller towns the choice is limited to staple dishes – mutton, kebabs, *couscous* and the like. In the caravanseries of the south, food is not so good. Local wines, not always obtainable, are cheap but sometimes heavy. A popular alternative is mint tea.

Trains, taxis and buses are adequate. In hire cars you can reach interesting places without straying from a metaled road. It is worth taking a look at the Sahara, but preferably with a local driver and a guide in a properly equipped vehicle.

Ait Benhaddou: a tribal citadel *above.* 'Ait' means 'children of' and is a common prefix to Moroccan names. Benhaddou must have been a mountain chieftain or patriarch or the Mr Big of a farming community. This is the *kasbah* (fortified habitation, more than a house but less than a village) which secured Benhaddou's family and dependants against interference from plundering nomads or predatory neighbors. Such *kasbahs* are sprinkled all over southern Morocco, on strategic sites chosen for their defensive qualities and good visibility. Generally they command a seasonal watercourse at the entrance to a mountain pass. Nearly all are now deserted.

Marrakesh: dyed woollens emblazon the suq *right*. The tourist authority provides an escort for the medina of Marrakesh; even those who live there sometimes get lost. But in the old *kasbah* area, near the royal palaces and the Saadian tombs, there is a simpler tangle of lanes and shops, bewildering only in the scents and sounds issuing from its curious trades and commodities. Dyed garments of wool and goats' hair emblazon this street, while the brass-workers and copper-beaters maintain a continual fanfare.

Morocco's green hills and cooling streams *left*. Not many miles away the Sahara begins and water costs more than whisky. But here are forests of oak and pine and cedar, grassy sheep pastures, destructive torrents dashing their waters recklessly over bush and rock. Here in the foothills of the Atlas (highest peak 13,352 feet) deep snow is common and in winter some of the Berber villages have to be supplied by helicopter. In Greek mythology the giant Atlas was sentenced to stay here for ever, supporting the heavens with his upraised hands.

Index

Acknowledgements

The publishers thank the following for providing the photographs in this book:
The Photo Source/CLI 11 below, 14, 21, 22–23, 27, 28, 29 below, 36, below, 38, 54–55, 59, 63 below; Zefa Picture Library 1, 2–3, 4–5, 6–7, 8–9, 10, 11 above, 12–13, 13, 15, 16, 17, 18–19, 19, 20–21, 24–25, 26, 29 above, 30, 31, 32–33, 34–35, 36 above, 37, 39, 40, 40–41, 42–43, 44–45, 46, 46–47, 48, 48–49, 50, 51, 52–53, 53, 56–57, 58–59, 60, 61, 62, 63 above.